LIZ CHENEY

The Woman Who Took on Trump

by

Leola Allison

Legal Note

No part of this book may be reproduced or transmitted in any form or by any means, electronic or mechanical, including photocopying, recording, or by any information storage and retrieval system, without written permission from the author, except for the inclusion of brief quotations in a review.

Disclaimer

The author and publisher assume no responsibility for errors or omissions or for any consequences resulting from the use of the information contained herein. The information provided in this book is for general informational purposes only. The author and publisher assume no responsibility for errors, inaccuracies, or omissions. Readers are encouraged to verify any information before relying on it.

Copyright © 2024 by Leola Allison. All rights reserved.

Table of Contents

Introduction 4
    Chapter 1 6
In the Shadow of Legacy 6
    Chapter 2: 9
Forging Her Own Path 9
    Chapter 3: 13
Iron Lady of Wyoming 13
    Chapter 4: 17
A Seat at the Table 17
    Chapter 5: 22
Defiance and Conviction 22
    Chapter 6: 26
The Rise of Trumpism 26
    Chapter 7: 31
Clash of Titans 31
    Chapter 8: 36
The Acquittal and the Fallout 36
    Chapter 9: 41
An Uncomfortable Spotlight 41

Chapter 10: 46
Voices of Support 46
Chapter 11: 52
The Party Divided 52
Chapter 12: 58
The Wyoming Dilemma 58
Chapter 13: 64
Legacy of Courage 64
Chapter 14: 69
The Future of the GOP 69
Chapter 15: 75
The Unfinished Story 75
Conclusion: Defiance, Legacy, and the Power of Conviction 80

Introduction:

Defiance in the Halls of Power

In the hallowed corridors of Washington, where whispers of influence intertwine with the echoes of history, emerges a figure whose iron will and political brilliance have left an indelible mark on the American political landscape. Liz Cheney, a name synonymous with courage and conviction, has become a formidable force in a world that often demands conformity.

As the sun sets on the grand stage of American politics, Liz Cheney stands at the center of a tumultuous narrative, a narrative that unfolds in the shadow of a once towering figure – Donald J. Trump. In this gripping biography, we embark on a journey through the life of a woman who, with unwavering determination, carved her own path in the hallowed halls of power, defying the norms and challenging the status quo.

The pages that follow will unveil a riveting saga—one that not only traces Liz Cheney's meteoric rise but also explores the crucible of her recent political battles with none other than the 45th President of the United States, Donald Trump. It is a clash of titans, a clash that reverberates through the core of the Republican Party, shaking the foundations of loyalty and challenging the very essence of conservatism.

In these chapters, we will peel back the layers of Liz Cheney's life, laying bare the motivations, struggles, and triumphs that have defined her journey. From the corridors of power in Wyoming to the heart of the nation's capital, we will witness a woman who fearlessly confronted the storm, standing resolute in the face of political tempests.

As the political drama unfolds, we delve into the intricacies of Cheney's defiance against the currents of Trumpism, an act that sparked a political wildfire, transforming her into a lightning rod for controversy within her own party. It's a tale of resilience and conviction that challenges preconceived notions, forcing us to confront the complex intersection of ideology, loyalty, and the relentless pursuit of truth.

So, dear reader, fasten your seatbelts as we embark on a journey through the corridors of power with Liz Cheney—a woman who, against all odds, stood firm in the face of political tumult, etching her name into the annals of American history. The stage is set, the stakes are high, and the drama is about to unfold. Welcome to the world of Liz Cheney: The Woman Who Took on Trump.

Chapter 1

In the Shadow of Legacy

Early Years in Wyoming: Exploring the roots of Liz Cheney and the political dynasty that shaped her upbringing.

In the vast expanse of the Wyoming landscape, where the echoes of political history reverberate through the rugged mountains and expansive plains, a young Liz Cheney began her journey—forging an identity that would be forever entwined with the weighty legacy of the Cheney name.

On a sweltering July day in 1966, amidst the buzz of political intrigue in Madison, Wisconsin, Elizabeth Lynne Cheney arrived, destined to forge her own path in the shadow of power. Her father, Dick Cheney, a stalwart figure in American politics, was already making his mark as a promising leader. But it was Wyoming, with its vast, windswept plains and the unwavering resilience of its people that truly molded young Liz.

The Cheney family moved to Casper, Wyoming, when Liz was just a child, and it was amidst the untamed beauty of the American West that she began to understand the significance of her family's political lineage. Her father's political aspirations propelled the family into the heart of Wyoming's political circles, casting a shadow that would both guide and challenge the course of Liz's life.

The Cheney name, synonymous with conservative values and unyielding principles, became Liz's inheritance and burden. Early on, it was evident that she was no stranger to the intricacies of political life. Dinner conversations often revolved around policy debates, and the hallways of the Cheney household echoed with the footsteps of statesmen.

Liz's formative years in Wyoming were marked by a unique blend of privilege and expectation. She attended Natrona County High School in Casper, where her intelligence and leadership skills began to shine. The young Cheney was not content merely to rest on the laurels of her family name; instead, she emerged as a formidable force in her own right.

The wild landscapes of Wyoming served as a canvas for Liz's early ambitions, but they also harbored a sense of duty. As her father climbed the political ladder—eventually becoming the Secretary of Defense under President George H.W. Bush—Liz Cheney found herself navigating the delicate balance between the expectations placed upon her and the desire to carve her own path.

In the years leading up to her departure for college, Liz's worldview expanded beyond the borders of Wyoming. Attending Colorado College and later the University of Chicago Law School, she absorbed knowledge and honed her skills, laying the foundation for the journey that awaited her.

As we embark on this exploration of Liz Cheney's early years in Wyoming, we peel back the layers of a political legacy that cast a long shadow over her formative experiences. The untamed spirit of the West, coupled with the weight of familial expectations, laid the groundwork for the woman who would later stand defiantly against the tide of Trumpism—an iconoclast rooted deeply in the legacy of the Cheney name.

Chapter 2:

Forging Her Own Path

Coming of Age in Politics:
The early signs of Liz Cheney's political aspirations and her journey to establishing a unique identity within the Cheney dynasty.

In the political tapestry of the Cheney dynasty, the early signs of Liz Cheney's destiny were woven with threads of ambition, intellect, and a determination to carve out a distinct identity within the formidable shadow of her family's legacy. As we delve into the annals of Liz's formative years, we encounter a young woman whose political awakening mirrored the fervent landscapes of her beloved Wyoming.

The journey to forging her own path began in earnest during Liz's college years at Colorado College, where she immersed herself in the study of international relations. The early 1980s marked a period of significant geopolitical tension, with the Cold War at its zenith, and Liz's academic pursuits were not just a quest for knowledge but a reflection of the global complexities that would later shape her political outlook.

Graduating with honors in 1988, Liz Cheney's journey into the political arena gained momentum. Her academic prowess laid the groundwork for what would become a distinguished career, but it was the call to public service that set her on a trajectory beyond the confines of lecture halls and textbooks. The seeds of political aspiration, firmly planted during her formative years, began to sprout.

The year 1989 saw Liz Cheney join the United States Agency for International Development (USAID), where she worked on projects in Poland and Czechoslovakia. This early exposure to the world of international relations and diplomacy not only fortified her understanding of global affairs but also nurtured the seeds of leadership that would later bloom on the domestic front.

As the 1990s unfolded, so did Liz's commitment to public service. The fall of the Berlin Wall and the subsequent dissolution of the Soviet Union heralded a new era, and Liz found herself at the epicenter of historical change. Her role at the State Department, where she focused on Eastern European democracy initiatives, showcased her ability to navigate complex geopolitical landscapes—an early indicator of the strategic acumen that would become a hallmark of her political career.

However, forging her own path wasn't merely about navigating international affairs. The Cheney legacy loomed large, and Liz faced the challenge of establishing herself within a political dynasty known for its patriarchal prominence. The dynamics shifted when her father, Dick Cheney, assumed the role of Vice President under President George W. Bush in 2001.

Far from being overshadowed, Liz seized the opportunity to contribute her intellect and expertise to the national stage. She served as Deputy Assistant Secretary of State for Near Eastern Affairs under President Bush, honing her skills in matters of national security and foreign policy—a testament to her ability to thrive under the weight of familial expectations.

As the Bush administration grappled with the aftermath of the September 11 attacks, Liz Cheney's role became increasingly pivotal. Her unwavering commitment to national security, coupled with her articulate advocacy, marked her as a rising star within the corridors of power. It was during this period that the nation witnessed Liz Cheney emerging from the shadow of her family's legacy, not as a mere extension, but as a force in her own right

Her journey within the Cheney dynasty culminated with her appointment as Principal Deputy Assistant Secretary of State for the Middle East. The early signs of Liz's political aspirations had evolved into a full-fledged commitment to public service at the highest levels, proving that she was not content to rest on the laurels of her family name.

As the early 2000s unfolded, Liz Cheney's path continued to diverge from the conventional expectations associated with political legacies. In 2009, she founded the nonprofit organization, Keep America Safe, further solidifying her commitment to conservative principles and national security.

The stage was set for Liz Cheney to ascend to new heights, and her unique identity within the Cheney dynasty had been firmly established. From the landscapes of Wyoming to the global theater of diplomacy, she had not only forged her own path but had done so with a resolute determination that hinted at the political battles yet to come.

As we reflect on Liz Cheney's formative years, we witness the evolution of a woman whose early signs of political prowess transcended the familial confines of the Cheney dynasty. The coming of age in politics marked not just a personal journey but the emergence of a political force—a force that would later take on the highest echelons of power with an iron will and political brilliance unparalleled in contemporary American politics.

Chapter 3:

Iron Lady of Wyoming

Political Beginnings: Liz Cheney's ascent in Wyoming politics, navigating the challenges and expectations of being a Cheney.

As Liz Cheney set her sights on the expansive landscapes of Wyoming, she embarked on a political journey that would solidify her reputation as a tenacious and principled leader. The rugged beauty of the Cowboy State provided the backdrop for a chapter in Liz's life where she would navigate the intricate dance of politics, identity, and legacy.

The early 2000s marked a crucial juncture as Liz Cheney returned to her roots, seeking to make her mark on the political stage in the state that had shaped her formative years. The year 2012 witnessed her entry into the U.S. Senate race, a bid that would become a defining moment in her political career.

Wyoming, known for its independent spirit and conservative values, presented both a homecoming and a crucible for Liz Cheney. The expectations placed upon her, not only as a political aspirant but as a Cheney, were immense. The shadow of her father's political legacy loomed large, but Liz approached the challenge with an iron will and an unwavering commitment to the principles that had defined her upbringing.

Cheney's decision to run for the Senate was not solely about familial tradition; it was a declaration of her dedication to the people of Wyoming. As she crisscrossed the state, from Cheyenne to Jackson, Liz connected with voters on a personal level, sharing her vision for a Wyoming that echoed the values of hard work, independence, and a deep-rooted commitment to conservative ideals.

The Wyoming political landscape, while familiar to Liz, presented its own set of challenges. In a state where ranching traditions and a love for the outdoors are as entrenched as the mountain ranges, earning the trust and respect of constituents required more than just a familiar last name. Liz Cheney, however, rose to the occasion, articulating a vision for Wyoming that blended tradition with a forward-looking approach.

The campaign trail in Wyoming was a rugged one, mirroring the untamed wilderness that defines the state. The challenges ranged from addressing concerns about her ties to Washington, D.C., to navigating the delicate balance of being a Cheney in a state that values individualism. Yet, Liz's innate ability to connect with people, coupled with her deep understanding of the state's unique character, proved to be formidable assets.

As the months unfolded, Liz Cheney's political acumen became increasingly evident. Her campaign garnered support from a diverse cross-section of Wyoming's population, signaling not just an acceptance but an embrace of her vision for the state. Town hall meetings in Cody and Laramie became platforms for Liz to articulate her commitment to Wyoming's economic prosperity, its energy industry, and the preservation of its natural beauty.

The Wyoming Senate race was not just about securing a seat; it was a test of Liz Cheney's ability to bridge the gap between the familial legacy she carried and the expectations of a state known for its fierce independence. The primary election in August 2012 was a pivotal moment, and as the results rolled in, it became clear that Liz Cheney had successfully navigated the challenges, securing the Republican nomination.

However, the political journey in Wyoming was not without its twists and turns. The path to the Senate seat faced hurdles, including the scrutiny of opponents and media, but Liz's resilience shone through. It was a testament to the iron will forged in the Wyoming wilderness and the political brilliance honed through years of public service.

The general election in November 2012 painted Wyoming in shades of red, as Liz Cheney emerged victorious, becoming the state's U.S. Senate nominee. Her ascent in Wyoming politics was not merely a triumph for the Cheney legacy but a testament to her ability to transcend familial expectations and resonate with the people she sought to represent.

As Liz Cheney's political star rose in Wyoming, it became evident that she was not just the daughter of a former Vice President; she was the Iron Lady of Wyoming—a title earned through grit, determination, and an unwavering commitment to the principles she held dear. The challenges of being a Cheney in Wyoming's political landscape had become the crucible that forged a leader ready to confront the even greater battles that lay ahead. The woman who had carved her own path had, indeed, etched her name into the political history of Wyoming, setting the stage for the chapters that would follow in her remarkable journey.

Chapter 4:

A Seat at the Table

Congressional Odyssey: The dynamics of Liz Cheney's entry into the U.S. House of Representatives and her impact on the national political stage.

As the sun dipped below the Wyoming horizon, casting long shadows over the sweeping landscapes, Liz Cheney's political journey took an unforeseen turn. The next chapter of her odyssey unfolded not within the bounds of the Cowboy State but within the hallowed halls of the United States Capitol—a realm where power and influence converged, and where Liz Cheney would leave an indelible mark on the national political stage.

The pivotal moment arrived in 2016, as Liz Cheney made the decision to run for Wyoming's lone seat in the U.S. House of Representatives. The echoes of her Senate campaign still resonated through the state, but this new endeavor marked a shift in both scale and scope. The dynamics of this Congressional odyssey were shaped by the intricate interplay of Wyoming's political landscape and the broader currents of a nation in flux.

Wyoming, with its sparse population and vast expanses, had always held a unique position in the tapestry of American politics. For Liz Cheney, entering the race for the House seat meant navigating the nuances of representing a state known for its independence while also influencing the broader trajectory of the nation. The stakes were high, and the challenges formidable.

The campaign trail crisscrossed Wyoming, from the historic trails of Independence Rock to the bustling energy hubs of Casper and Gillette. Liz Cheney, in her trademark cowboy boots and with an unwavering resolve, connected with voters on issues ranging from energy policy to rural healthcare. Her commitment to conservative values and her deep understanding of Wyoming's economic landscape resonated with a diverse array of constituents.

The primary election in August 2016 became a milestone in Liz Cheney's Congressional odyssey. The Republican nomination secured, she faced limited opposition in the general election, reflecting not just the state's Republican stronghold but also the resonance of her message with Wyomingites. On January 3, 2017, Liz Cheney was sworn in as Wyoming's Representative in the U.S. House.

Stepping into the historic chambers of the House of Representatives, Liz Cheney carried with her not just the hopes of Wyoming but also a legacy that stretched across generations. The Cheney name had found a place within the walls where legislative decisions shaped the course of the nation. The dynamics of her entry into the House were not merely about claiming a seat; they were about asserting a voice—a voice that echoed the principles ingrained in the Cheney DNA.

The early days in Congress were a whirlwind of activity for Liz Cheney. Her committees and assignments reflected a focus on national security, echoing her earlier roles at the State Department. As a member of the House Armed Services Committee and the Natural Resources Committee, she brought a unique blend of expertise that transcended the boundaries of domestic and international affairs.

The year 2019 marked another significant milestone in Liz Cheney's Congressional journey. With the resignation of Representative Liz Cheney took the reins as the Chair of the House Republican Conference—a position that catapulted her into the forefront of party leadership. The dynamics of her role were not confined to legislative matters; they extended to the very heart of the Republican Party's identity and messaging.

In this capacity, Liz Cheney became a vocal advocate for conservative principles, a staunch defender of American exceptionalism, and a forceful critic of policies she deemed detrimental to the nation's security. Her impact on the national political stage was magnified as she assumed a prominent role in shaping the Republican Party's response to the challenges of the day.

The dynamics of Liz Cheney's Congressional odyssey were shaped not just by legislative maneuvering but also by her principled stands on issues that transcended party lines. Her commitment to the Constitution, her advocacy for a robust national defense, and her unwavering support for conservative values marked her as a formidable presence in the House.

The national political stage became a theater where Liz Cheney's influence reverberated, shaping conversations and debates on critical issues. From the intricacies of foreign policy to the challenges of energy independence, she emerged as a thought leader within the Republican Party—a status earned not just through her lineage but through a meticulous dedication to the intricacies of governance.

As Liz Cheney's Congressional odyssey unfolded, it became clear that her impact was not confined to Wyoming. Her voice resonated beyond the rolling hills of the West, reaching the far corners of the nation. The dynamics of her entry into the U.S. House of Representatives were not just about claiming a seat at the table; they were about redefining the contours of conservative leadership in a rapidly evolving political landscape.

The story of Liz Cheney's Congressional journey is one of navigating the complex currents of Capitol Hill, of asserting principles forged in the Wyoming wilderness on the national stage. As we turn the pages of this chapter, we witness the emergence of a leader who not only carved her own path but who, with an iron will and political brilliance, left an indelible mark on the halls of power—a mark that would become even more pronounced in the tumultuous chapters that lay ahead.

Chapter 5:

Defiance and Conviction

The Unyielding Principles: A deep dive into Liz Cheney's political principles and the early signs of her willingness to defy party norms.

In the labyrinth of Washington's political landscape, where party loyalty often eclipses individual conviction, Liz Cheney emerged as a beacon of unyielding principles. As we delve into this chapter, we explore the bedrock of her political identity—the core values and convictions that propelled her into the spotlight and set the stage for a political journey marked by defiance and unwavering commitment.

From the early stages of her political career, Liz Cheney exhibited a deep reverence for the principles that guided her decision-making. Born into a family with a storied legacy in conservative politics, she embraced a set of values rooted in the ethos of limited government, individual liberties, and a strong national defense. These principles were not merely inherited; they were internalized, becoming the compass that directed her path in the tumultuous realm of American politics.

The early signs of Liz Cheney's willingness to defy party norms emerged during her tenure as Wyoming's Representative in the U.S. House of Representatives. While party loyalty often dictates the actions of lawmakers, Cheney's commitment to the Constitution and her vision for a principled conservatism transcended partisan lines. Her legislative record mirrored a dedication to the values she held dear, even when it meant challenging the prevailing sentiments within her own party.

One defining aspect of Cheney's unyielding principles was her steadfast commitment to a robust national defense. Her role on the House Armed Services Committee wasn't just a position; it was a platform from which she advocated for a military that could protect the nation's interests on the global stage. Her insistence on adequate defense funding and a strategic approach to international challenges marked her as a leading voice on matters of national security.

As we navigate the intricate corridors of this chapter, it becomes apparent that Liz Cheney's defiance wasn't born out of mere contrarianism but out of a sincere belief that transcended political expediency. Whether it was her opposition to the Obama administration's nuclear deal with Iran or her push for a more assertive stance against Russian aggression, Cheney's positions were informed by a commitment to the preservation of American interests and values.

Her willingness to defy party norms became particularly evident during the presidency of Donald J. Trump. The year 2016 marked a seismic shift in American politics, as Trump, an unconventional figure, ascended to the highest office in the land. Cheney's principled conservatism collided with the uncharted territories of Trumpism, setting the stage for a clash of ideologies within the Republican Party.

The early signs of Cheney's defiance crystallized during Trump's candidacy when she voiced concerns about his temperament and questioned his commitment to conservative principles. As the Republican nominee and later as President, Trump's unconventional approach to governance often diverged from the traditional conservative playbook. Cheney, undeterred by party pressure, continued to speak out when she perceived a departure from the principles that had defined her political upbringing.

The watershed moment came in 2017 when Liz Cheney, now a prominent member of the House Republican leadership, took a stand on a matter of profound significance. In the aftermath of the deadly white supremacist rally in Charlottesville, Virginia, Trump's response drew criticism from various quarters. Cheney, breaking from the reticence of some within her party, unequivocally condemned the president's equivocal remarks, reaffirming her commitment to moral clarity and the rejection of bigotry.

This instance illuminated the depth of Cheney's conviction—a conviction that transcended the partisan divide and underscored her belief in the moral compass that should guide the nation's leaders. It became a hallmark of her political identity—a willingness to confront uncomfortable truths and challenge party norms when the principles she held dear were at stake.

As the pages of this chapter turn, we witness the unfolding of a political narrative that showcases Liz Cheney's defiance not as an act of rebellion but as a manifestation of deeply held convictions. The unyielding principles that guided her were not confined to mere rhetoric; they found expression in her actions, even when those actions set her on a collision course with powerful forces within her own party.

This chapter is a journey into the crucible of Cheney's political principles—a crucible that tested the mettle of her convictions and laid the groundwork for the seismic clashes that would follow. From the early signs of her willingness to defy party norms, a portrait emerges of a leader whose commitment to principles would set the stage for one of the most consequential battles in modern American politics.

Chapter 6:

The Rise of Trumpism

The Political Landscape Shifts: Examining the emergence of Donald Trump and its impact on the Republican Party, setting the stage for future conflicts.

In the annals of American political history, few phenomena have been as seismic as the rise of Donald Trump. The landscape of the Republican Party, once characterized by established norms and traditions, underwent a profound shift in the early 21st century. As we navigate through this chapter, we unravel the complex tapestry of Trumpism—a political force that would shape the trajectory of the nation and set the stage for a clash of ideologies, with Liz Cheney emerging as a central figure in this unfolding drama.

The roots of Trumpism can be traced back to the year 2015 when Donald Trump, a brash businessman and reality TV personality, announced his candidacy for the presidency. The political establishment viewed his entrance into the race with skepticism, dismissing it as a quixotic endeavor. However, as the campaign gained momentum, it became evident that Trump's unorthodox approach to politics resonated with a significant segment of the electorate.

The primary elections of 2016 marked a turning point. State after state fell into the Trump column, and the conventional wisdom of political pundits crumbled. In July 2016, at the Republican National Convention in Cleveland, Ohio, Trump secured the party's nomination, signaling a seismic shift in the GOP's identity.

Trumpism, as a political ideology, was marked by a rejection of traditional conservative orthodoxy. Populist in nature, it emphasized economic nationalism, anti-globalism, and a confrontational approach to issues such as immigration. The political landscape, once defined by the likes of Ronald Reagan and George W. Bush, was now being reshaped by the unfiltered rhetoric and unapologetic style of Donald Trump.

The impact of Trump's ascendancy on the Republican Party was profound. Divisions emerged between establishment Republicans, who were often uneasy with Trump's unorthodox methods, and a growing faction of the party that embraced the president's disruptive approach. This internal schism laid the groundwork for future conflicts within the GOP, setting the stage for a battle over the party's soul.

Liz Cheney, situated within the party's leadership, found herself at the epicenter of this political earthquake. Her commitment to conservative principles, forged in the crucible of her Wyoming upbringing, collided with the populist wave of Trumpism. As Trump secured the presidency in November 2016, Cheney faced the challenge of navigating a political landscape where loyalty to the president often trumped traditional party ideology.

The early signs of conflict emerged as the Trump administration unfolded its policy agenda. Cheney, while supportive of certain conservative policies, did not shy away from expressing reservations when she perceived departures from long-standing Republican principles. The push for protectionist trade policies, the controversial travel ban, and the handling of relations with Russia were points of contention that hinted at the ideological fault lines within the party.

The year 2017 witnessed the first major test of Cheney's commitment to principle over party loyalty. In August, white supremacists and neo-Nazis staged a violent rally in Charlottesville, Virginia. President Trump's response, which included statements equating white supremacists with counter-protesters, drew widespread condemnation. In a notable act of defiance, Cheney publicly criticized the president's remarks, emphasizing the need for moral clarity and a rejection of hate.

This moment set the stage for a recurring theme in Cheney's political journey—the willingness to confront uncomfortable truths and challenge party norms when principles were at stake. The clash between the traditional conservatism embodied by Cheney and the populist fervor of Trumpism became more pronounced, setting the stage for a larger ideological battle within the Republican Party.

The dynamics within the GOP reached a boiling point in 2019 with the impeachment proceedings against President Trump. The House of Representatives, led by Democrats, charged Trump with abuse of power and obstruction of Congress related to his dealings with Ukraine. Cheney, as the Chair of the House Republican Conference, faced a pivotal moment that would test her allegiance to both party and principle.

In December 2019, as the articles of impeachment reached the House floor, Liz Cheney broke ranks with the majority of her party, voting in favor of impeaching President Trump. It was a decision that reverberated through the political landscape, signaling a willingness to prioritize constitutional principles over partisan loyalty. The move, while garnering praise from some quarters for its principled stance, also intensified the internal divisions within the Republican Party.

The rise of Trumpism had set the stage for a clash of ideologies that extended beyond policy disagreements. It became a battle for the soul of the GOP, a struggle between the traditional conservatism represented by figures like Liz Cheney and the populist, anti-establishment sentiment championed by Trump and his supporters.

As this chapter unfolds, we witness the early signs of Cheney's defiance against the tide of Trumpism. The political landscape, reshaped by the seismic force of Donald Trump's presidency, becomes a battleground where principles and party loyalty collide. The stage is set for a political drama that will play out in the chapters to come, with Liz Cheney emerging as a central protagonist in the unfolding narrative of a party at a crossroads.

Chapter 7:

Clash of Titans

Liz vs. Trump: Unraveling the complexities of Liz Cheney's clashes with Donald Trump and the ideological battleground that ensued.

The political arena of the early 2020s became a stage for a clash of titans—the unyielding Liz Cheney and the formidable force of Donald Trump's influence. As we delve into this chapter, we unravel the complexities of their clashes, navigating through the ideological battleground that unfolded against the backdrop of a nation in flux.

The contours of this conflict began to take shape in the aftermath of the impeachment proceedings in 2019. Liz Cheney's vote in favor of impeaching President Trump sent shockwaves through the Republican Party. As the nation braced for the 2020 elections, the ideological fault lines within the GOP became more pronounced, setting the stage for a showdown between Cheney's commitment to principles and Trump's grip on the party's base.

The year 2020, dominated by the challenges of the COVID-19 pandemic, witnessed the convergence of divergent political forces. As the nation grappled with a public health crisis, the presidential election loomed on the horizon, further intensifying the political tumult. Trump, seeking re-election, presented a vision rooted in populism and a rejection of traditional norms. Cheney, now a prominent figure in the party, continued to champion a more traditional conservative platform.

The clash between Liz Cheney and Donald Trump became increasingly public and played out on multiple fronts. Trump, through his prolific use of social media, exerted influence over the party's messaging and direction. Cheney, as a member of the House Republican leadership, found herself navigating a delicate balance—upholding her conservative principles while acknowledging the potency of Trump's sway over a significant segment of the Republican base.

The ideological battleground reached a crescendo in the aftermath of the 2020 presidential election. As Trump, despite legal challenges, refused to concede defeat to Joe Biden, Cheney broke ranks with many in her party by acknowledging the legitimacy of the election results. Her public stance, a departure from Trump's claims of widespread voter fraud, marked a watershed moment in the clash of ideologies

The fallout was swift and dramatic. Trump, through his preferred mode of communication, took to Twitter to criticize Cheney and other Republicans who dared to question the integrity of the election. The ideological battleground shifted from policy disagreements to a fundamental question—loyalty to the leader versus fidelity to the democratic process.

Cheney's unwavering commitment to the truth and constitutional principles stood in stark contrast to Trump's refusal to accept the election outcome. The clash of titans escalated as Trump's influence within the party clashed with Cheney's determination to uphold the principles she deemed fundamental to the conservative cause.

The events of January 6, 2021, at the U.S. Capitol, added a new layer of complexity to the ideological battleground. As a mob of Trump supporters stormed the Capitol in an attempt to overturn the election results, Cheney condemned the violence in unequivocal terms. She laid the blame squarely at the feet of the then-President, further deepening the schism within the Republican Party.

The aftermath of the Capitol riot underscored the profound divisions within the GOP. While some Republicans sought to distance themselves from Trump in the wake of the violence, others remained steadfast in their allegiance. Liz Cheney emerged as a leading voice calling for accountability and a reckoning with the events of that fateful day, setting the stage for a clash with Trump loyalists.

In the ensuing months, Cheney continued to be a vocal critic of Trump's role in the Capitol attack and his refusal to accept responsibility. Her stance, while earning praise from some quarters for its moral clarity, drew the ire of Trump and his allies. The clash of titans, now played out in the public arena, became a defining narrative within the Republican Party.

As the GOP grappled with its identity post-Trump, Cheney's clashes with the former President took center stage. Trump, through endorsements and public statements, sought to undermine Cheney's standing within the party, labeling her a "warmonger" and endorsing primary challengers to her Wyoming congressional seat. Cheney, undeterred by the political headwinds, stood her ground, cementing her status as a bulwark against what she perceived as a departure from conservative principles.

The ideological battleground, marked by clashes over the election, the Capitol riot, and the direction of the Republican Party, reached a critical juncture when Cheney faced a challenge to her leadership position in the House Republican Conference. In May 2021, a faction of Republicans sought to oust her from the leadership role, citing her refusal to align with the party's prevailing sentiments. The vote, a litmus test for the GOP's direction, ultimately resulted in Cheney's removal from leadership—a move widely seen as a victory for Trumpism within the party.

The clash of titans, while marked by political maneuvering and strategic battles, was ultimately a struggle for the soul of the Republican Party. Liz Cheney's unwavering commitment to conservative principles, even in the face of intense political pressure, positioned her as a symbol of resistance against the populist tide of Trumpism. The ideological battleground, though fraught with challenges and setbacks, showcased Cheney's iron will and political brilliance in confronting a force that had reshaped the political landscape.

As we turn the pages of this chapter, we witness the clash of titans—the woman who took on Trump, challenging the very essence of Trumpism within the GOP. The ideological battleground, far from being a mere arena for policy disputes, became a testing ground for the resilience of principles and the ability of a leader to stand firm in the face of political storms. The narrative unfolds against the backdrop of a nation grappling with its identity, and Liz Cheney emerges as a central figure in this gripping tale of ideological conflict and political resilience.

Chapter 8:

The Acquittal and the Fallout

Impeachment Drama: Analyzing Liz Cheney's stance during the Trump impeachment trials and the subsequent fallout within the Republican Party.

As the nation grappled with the aftermath of the Capitol riot on January 6, 2021, the specter of impeachment loomed large over the political landscape. The House of Representatives, led by Democrats, swiftly moved to charge then-President Donald Trump with incitement of insurrection. This set the stage for a historic second impeachment trial, and in the center of this political maelstrom stood Liz Cheney, a prominent figure in the Republican Party and a vocal critic of Trump's role in the events that unfolded on that fateful day.

The impeachment drama unfolded against a backdrop of heightened tension and a deeply divided nation. The House of Representatives, where Cheney held a leadership position as the Chair of the House Republican Conference, became the arena for a high-stakes battle over the accountability of a sitting president. As the proceedings commenced, Cheney's stance on the impeachment trials became a defining moment that would reverberate through the Republican Party.

The House, in a bipartisan vote, impeached Trump for incitement of insurrection on January 13, 2021. Cheney, breaking with a majority of her party, emerged as one of ten House Republicans who voted in favor of impeachment. Her decision, rooted in her conviction that Trump bore responsibility for the Capitol riot, marked a bold departure from prevailing sentiments within the GOP.

Cheney's stance during the impeachment trials showcased a commitment to principle that transcended political calculations. In a statement released on the day of the vote, she articulated her rationale, asserting that there had never been a greater betrayal by a President of the United States of his office and his oath to the Constitution. Her words echoed with the clarity of a leader unswayed by partisan considerations, willing to confront uncomfortable truths for the sake of preserving the integrity of the nation's democratic institutions.

The fallout from Cheney's decision was swift and intense. Trump, now a private citizen after leaving office, responded with a scathing rebuke, labeling Cheney and other Republicans who voted for impeachment as "Republican in name only" (RINOs). The former President, who retained a considerable influence over the party base, signaled his intention to challenge those who dared to defy him, setting the stage for a battle within the GOP.

The rift within the Republican Party widened as Cheney's stance during the impeachment trials became a flashpoint for internal discord. Traditional conservatives, appreciative of her principled stand, found themselves at odds with the Trump loyalists who dominated certain factions of the party. The ideological fault lines, already pronounced, now threatened to fracture the GOP into competing camps—those who adhered to the principles of conservatism and constitutional accountability, and those who remained steadfast in their allegiance to Trump.

The Republican National Committee (RNC) meeting in February 2021 became a microcosm of the internal tensions. Cheney faced a censure motion from the Wyoming Republican Party for her vote on impeachment, highlighting the deep divisions within her home state. The censure, while symbolic, underscored the challenges Cheney confronted within her own party—a party that was undergoing a profound identity crisis in the aftermath of Trump's presidency.

Cheney's resilience in the face of political headwinds became a defining characteristic during this tumultuous period. She continued to assert her position, defending her vote on impeachment as a matter of conscience and constitutional duty. The fallout from her decision, however, extended beyond party politics and had tangible consequences for her leadership role within the House Republican Conference.

In May 2021, the internal strife within the party reached a climax when Cheney faced a challenge to her position as the Chair of the House Republican Conference. A faction of Republicans, aligning with Trump's vision for the party, sought to remove Cheney from her leadership role. The vote, conducted behind closed doors, resulted in Cheney's ousting—a development that sent shockwaves through the political landscape and underscored the ascendancy of Trumpism within the GOP.

The fallout from Cheney's stance during the impeachment trials revealed the deep-seated challenges facing the Republican Party. The battle between adherence to conservative principles and loyalty to Trump's legacy became a defining narrative, and Cheney emerged as a casualty of this ideological struggle. The party, at a crossroads, grappled with the question of whether it would remain anchored in traditional conservative values or continue down the path forged by Trump's populist movement.

As the curtain falls on this chapter, the impeachment drama and its aftermath lay bare the complexities of Liz Cheney's political journey. Her unwavering commitment to constitutional principles, even at the cost of personal and political consequences, showcased a rare courage in a political landscape fraught with partisanship. The fallout within the Republican Party, while marking a setback for Cheney's leadership within the GOP, set the stage for broader questions about the direction of the party and the role of principled conservatism in the post-Trump era. The clash of ideals, as embodied in Cheney's stance, became a harbinger of the challenges that lay ahead as the Republican Party grappled with its identity in a rapidly evolving political landscape.

Chapter 9:

An Uncomfortable Spotlight

Media Scrutiny: Liz Cheney's navigation through media attention, public scrutiny, and the pressures of being a prominent dissenting voice.

The journey of Liz Cheney through the halls of power has been one marked not only by the intricacies of politics but also by the unrelenting gaze of the media. As a prominent dissenting voice within the Republican Party, her every move and statement have been scrutinized under an unforgiving spotlight. In this chapter, we unravel the complexities of Liz Cheney's navigation through media attention, public scrutiny, and the unique pressures of being a principled figure in a political landscape often defined by polarization.

From her early years in Wyoming politics to her pivotal role in the national stage, Liz Cheney has been no stranger to the media spotlight. Born into a family with a political legacy, she grew up accustomed to the glare of public attention. However, it was her willingness to dissent from prevailing party sentiments, particularly regarding former President Donald Trump, that thrust her into an uncomfortable and often controversial spotlight.

The turning point came during the Trump presidency, when Cheney, as a member of the House Republican leadership, began to publicly voice her concerns about the direction of the party. Her critiques of Trump's policies, rhetoric, and his handling of key issues attracted both praise and condemnation. The media, always eager to capture the drama of internal party conflicts, turned its focus squarely on Cheney, transforming her into a central figure in the unfolding narrative of Republican dissent.

One of the defining moments of media scrutiny occurred during the impeachment drama in early 2021. Cheney's decision to vote in favor of impeaching Trump for his role in the Capitol riot was a move that reverberated through the media landscape. News outlets, both conservative and liberal, seized upon the drama of a high-profile Republican breaking ranks with the party. Cheney found herself in the eye of a political storm, with news cycles dominated by analyses of her motives, interviews seeking her perspective, and op-eds dissecting the implications of her stance.

The media scrutiny intensified as Cheney faced the fallout from her impeachment vote. The narrative of a party divided, torn between traditional conservatism and the influence of Trumpism, became a storyline that the imagination of journalists and political commentators. Cheney's press conferences, once routine affairs, turned into events where every word and nuance were dissected for potential implications on the broader Republican Party dynamics.

The uncomfortable spotlight extended beyond traditional news outlets to social media platforms. Cheney, an active user of Twitter, found herself engaged in a public dialogue where supporters and critics alike voiced their opinions with unprecedented immediacy. The platform, known for its polarized discourse, became both a tool for Cheney to articulate her principles and a battleground where her detractors sought to undermine her credibility.

The pressures of being a prominent dissenting voice were not confined to the virtual realm. Cheney's public appearances, whether on news programs or at events in her home state of Wyoming, became arenas where the complexities of her political stance were laid bare. Journalists probed, constituents questioned, and political opponents sought to capitalize on the discomfort that dissent within the ranks often brings.

The media's focus on Cheney extended beyond her policy positions to her personal life. Profiles and features delved into her upbringing, her relationship with her famous father, former Vice President Dick Cheney, and the challenges of being a woman in the male-dominated world of politics. The personal became intertwined with the political, adding an extra layer of complexity to the media's portrayal of Cheney as a central figure in the unfolding narrative of Republican dissent.

The dynamics of media scrutiny also intersected with gender dynamics. As a woman in politics, Cheney faced a unique set of challenges and expectations. The media, at times, scrutinized not only her policy positions but also her demeanor, attire, and even her tone of voice. The uncomfortable spotlight became a lens through which broader discussions about gender and power in politics were refracted, making Cheney not only a dissenting voice within the GOP but also a symbol of the evolving role of women in political leadership.

Navigating this uncomfortable spotlight required a delicate balancing act. Cheney, with an iron will forged in the Wyoming wilderness, remained resolute in her commitment to principles, often using media appearances as platforms to articulate her views with clarity and conviction. Yet, the pressures of being a prominent dissenting voice took a toll. The constant scrutiny, the relentless questioning, and the often harsh criticisms tested the mettle of Cheney's resolve.

The media's role in shaping public perceptions was evident in the narrative that unfolded around Cheney's removal from her leadership position within the House Republican Conference. The coverage, while diverse in its perspectives, contributed to a broader narrative of a party increasingly defined by loyalty to Trump and the challenges faced by dissenting voices.

As we turn the pages of this chapter, the uncomfortable spotlight remains a central theme in Liz Cheney's political journey. Her navigation through media scrutiny, public attention, and the unique pressures of being a prominent dissenting voice showcases not only the complexities of contemporary politics but also the resilience of a leader committed to principles in the face of intense scrutiny. The narrative unfolds against the backdrop of a media landscape that shapes and reflects the intricate dance between power, dissent, and the enduring quest for political integrity.

Chapter 10:

Voices of Support

Allies Amidst Adversity: Examining the individuals and groups that rallied behind Liz Cheney during her turbulent times.

In the crucible of political adversity, where dissent can be a lonely road, Liz Cheney found solace and strength in the voices of support that emerged from unexpected corners. This chapter delves into the tapestry of alliances that formed amidst the turbulence, examining the individuals and groups that rallied behind Cheney during some of the most challenging moments in her political journey.

One of the remarkable aspects of Liz Cheney's political resilience was the diverse array of voices that stood by her side. As she navigated the fallout from her impeachment vote and subsequent removal from House leadership, allies emerged from various spheres—political, ideological, and personal.

Fellow Republicans with Principles:

Amidst the waves of Trumpism that swept through the Republican Party, a cohort of fellow Republicans stood firmly with Liz Cheney, driven by a shared commitment to conservative principles. Senators such as Mitt Romney and Ben Sasse, along with a handful of House Republicans, openly voiced their support for Cheney's principled stand. They saw in her a guardian of traditional conservative values and a bulwark against the populist currents that threatened to redefine the party.

Romney, a prominent figure in the GOP and a former presidential nominee, lauded Cheney's courage in standing up for truth and the Constitution. Sasse, known for his independent voice within the party, echoed similar sentiments, emphasizing the need for leaders who prioritize principles over political expediency.

Conservative Commentators and Intellectuals:

Beyond the confines of Capitol Hill, conservative commentators and intellectuals added their voices to the chorus of support for Cheney. Writers and thinkers such as George Will, Jonah Goldberg, and David French, often critical of Trump's influence on the party, found in Cheney a champion for the enduring principles of conservatism.

These voices, whose influence extended through op-eds, articles, and televised commentary, provided a crucial platform for Cheney's message to reach a broader audience. Their support underscored the ideological battle within the Republican Party, framing Cheney not as an outlier but as a torchbearer for a conservatism rooted in constitutional fidelity and traditional values.

Legal Scholars and Constitutional Experts:

In the realm of legal and constitutional expertise, Cheney found allies who applauded her commitment to upholding the rule of law. Constitutional scholars like Laurence Tribe and legal analysts such as Jeffrey Toobin, despite their ideological differences with Cheney on many fronts, commended her for prioritizing constitutional principles over political expediency.

Tribe, a professor of constitutional law, highlighted Cheney's role in confronting the erosion of democratic norms and the rule of law. Toobin, a legal analyst with a broad audience, portrayed Cheney as a figure who, despite being a conservative, stood as a guardian of constitutional norms in a tumultuous political landscape.

Civil Rights Leaders and Advocates:

Beyond the conservative circles, voices from the realm of civil rights and advocacy recognized Cheney's efforts to confront the fallout from the Capitol riot and challenge the prevailing narrative within her party. Prominent figures like Van Jones, a civil rights advocate and CNN commentator, praised Cheney for her willingness to confront the racial undertones of the Capitol attack and the need for accountability.

Jones, known for his work on criminal justice reform and civil rights issues, saw in Cheney a partner in the pursuit of justice and accountability. Their unlikely alliance highlighted the cross-cutting nature of Cheney's support base, transcending traditional ideological divides.

Wyoming Constituents and Grassroots Support:

Closer to home, in the vast landscapes of Wyoming, Liz Cheney found enduring support from constituents who admired her principled stance. Grassroots organizations, often aligned with traditional conservative values and an emphasis on constitutional principles, rallied behind Cheney.

Despite the censure motion from the Wyoming Republican Party, a significant segment of the state's electorate voiced their support for Cheney's unwavering commitment to upholding the Constitution. Town halls and community gatherings became forums where Cheney's resilience resonated with those who valued a conservatism that transcended personality cults and focused on enduring principles.

As this chapter unfolds, it becomes evident that Liz Cheney's journey through the storm of political adversity was not a solitary one. Allies emerged from diverse quarters, united by a common thread—the recognition that, in the face of political turbulence, principles should prevail over expediency. Whether fellow Republicans, conservative commentators, legal scholars, civil rights leaders, or grassroots constituents, these voices of support formed a collective affirmation of Cheney's commitment to navigating the turbulent currents with an unwavering dedication to enduring principles.

The chorus of support, echoing through various channels, became a testament to the resilience of principled leadership in a political landscape often defined by polarization. In a time when dissent within party ranks was met with skepticism, Cheney's allies stood as a testament to the enduring power of conviction and the recognition that, in the realm of politics, principles are the anchor that withstands the storms of adversity. As the narrative unfolds, these voices of support play a crucial role in shaping the broader story of Liz Cheney—a woman who, amidst the political tempest, found allies in the unlikeliest of places, carving a path guided by iron will and an unwavering commitment to political brilliance.

Chapter 11:

The Party Divided

Impact on the GOP: Assessing the fractures within the Republican Party caused by Liz Cheney's principled stand against Trumpism.

In the annals of American politics, few chapters resonate with the echoes of internal strife as profoundly as the story of Liz Cheney's principled stand against Trumpism within the Republican Party. This chapter delves into the seismic impact her dissent has had on the GOP, assessing the fractures that emerged and reshaped the party's identity in the post-Trump era.

The year 2021 saw the Republican Party navigating treacherous waters, caught between the currents of traditional conservatism and the tidal wave of Trumpism. Liz Cheney, with her steadfast commitment to constitutional principles and unwavering condemnation of Donald Trump's actions, found herself at the epicenter of a political earthquake that reverberated through the GOP.

The Clash of Ideologies:

Cheney's principled stand against Trumpism exposed the fault lines that had been brewing within the Republican Party for years. The clash of ideologies, characterized by a struggle between traditional conservatism and the populist forces unleashed by Trump, became increasingly pronounced. Cheney's vocal dissent laid bare the deep-seated tensions within the GOP, raising fundamental questions about the party's identity and its future direction.

Traditional conservatives, who viewed Cheney as a standard-bearer for enduring principles, found themselves in direct conflict with the Trump loyalists who dominated certain factions of the party. The clash, marked by competing visions for the GOP, set the stage for a protracted battle over the soul of the party—a battle in which Cheney emerged as both a symbol and a casualty.

The Fractured Leadership:

Cheney's principled stand had immediate repercussions within the leadership ranks of the Republican Party. As a member of the House Republican leadership, holding the position of Chair of the House Republican Conference, her dissent placed her at odds with the prevailing sentiments of the party. The fractures within the leadership became glaringly evident as Cheney faced challenges to her position.

In May 2021, a faction of House Republicans sought to remove Cheney from her leadership role. The vote, conducted behind closed doors, reflected the internal divisions over loyalty to Trump and adherence to conservative principles. The outcome, Cheney's removal from leadership, underscored the ascendancy of Trumpism within the GOP and marked a turning point in the party's trajectory.

The Symbol of Resistance:

Cheney's principled stand against Trumpism elevated her to the status of a symbol of resistance within the Republican Party. Traditional conservatives, disheartened by what they perceived as a departure from core principles, rallied behind Cheney as a voice of reason and a defender of constitutional norms. Her stance became a rallying point for those who believed that the party should be rooted in conservative values rather than defined by loyalty to a singular personality.

As a symbol of resistance, Cheney became a focal point for conversations about the future of the Republican Party. Media outlets, political commentators, and grassroots organizers alike turned their attention to the impact of her dissent on the broader dynamics of the GOP. The narrative of a party divided, torn between loyalty to Trump and adherence to traditional conservative principles, unfolded with Cheney at its center.

Primary Challenges and Endorsements:

The fractures within the Republican Party manifested in the form of primary challenges and endorsements that underscored the battle for the party's direction. Cheney, facing backlash for her dissent, became the target of primary challengers endorsed by Trump and his allies. The endorsements signaled a broader shift within the GOP, where loyalty to Trump became a litmus test for political viability.

The primary challenges against Cheney in Wyoming, her home state, reflected the depth of the divisions. Trump's endorsements of her challengers, coupled with his public statements labeling Cheney as a "warmonger" and a "disappointment," galvanized a segment of the party base against her. The primary contests became battlegrounds where the ideological struggle within the GOP played out in real-time.

Public Opinion and Constituency Dynamics:

Cheney's principled stand against Trumpism also had repercussions at the grassroots level. Public opinion within the Republican base became polarized, with Cheney drawing both fierce support and vehement opposition. Town halls, traditionally spaces for elected officials to engage with constituents, transformed into arenas where the fractures within the party were palpable.

Constituency dynamics in Wyoming, a state where Cheney had deep political roots, showcased the challenges faced by a dissenting voice in a party increasingly defined by Trump's influence. The censure motion from the Wyoming Republican Party and the primary challenges reflected the intensifying struggle for the party's identity at the state level.

The Aftermath:

As this chapter unfolds, the aftermath of Liz Cheney's principled stand against Trumpism continues to shape the contours of the Republican Party. The fractures exposed by her dissent, though not entirely new, became more pronounced and laid bare the competing visions for the GOP's future. The impact on the party's identity, leadership dynamics, primary battles, and public opinion underscores the enduring significance of Cheney's role in this pivotal moment in American political history.

The story of the party divided, marked by the clash between traditional conservatism and Trumpism, unfolds against the backdrop of a nation grappling with its political identity. Cheney, with her iron will and political brilliance, emerges as a central figure in this narrative—a woman who, amidst the turbulence, dared to confront the forces reshaping the GOP and stood as a symbol of resistance against the tide of Trumpism. As we turn the pages, we witness the evolution of a party at a crossroads, navigating the complexities of dissent, loyalty, and the enduring quest for political integrity.

Chapter 12:

The Wyoming Dilemma

Political Backlash: The repercussions of Liz Cheney's stance on her political standing in Wyoming and the challenges she faced within her own constituency.

The vast expanse of Wyoming, with its sweeping landscapes and rugged terrain, has long been intertwined with the political legacy of the Cheney family. It is in this high-plains state, where the winds whisper through the sagebrush, that Liz Cheney faced a dilemma that echoed across the political landscape of her home state. The Wyoming Dilemma, as this chapter explores, delves into the intricate web of political backlash, challenging the very foundations of Cheney's standing within her constituency.

The Unforgiving Landscape:

Wyoming, a state known for its fiercely independent spirit and a deeply rooted conservative ethos, has been a stronghold of the Republican Party for decades. Against this backdrop, Liz Cheney's principled stand against Trumpism set in motion a political storm that reverberated through the very fabric of her political identity within the state.

The challenge lay not only in the ideological divisions but also in the visceral connection Wyomingites felt with the Cheney family. The Cheney name, synonymous with political influence and a legacy that reached the highest echelons of power, carried both weight and expectations. The unforgiving landscape of Wyoming politics, with its proud tradition of conservatism, presented a formidable challenge for Cheney as she navigated the aftermath of her dissent.

The Wyoming Republican Party's Censure:

The Wyoming Republican Party, a bastion of conservative values, became an arena where the Wyoming Dilemma played out in stark relief. In the wake of Liz Cheney's vote to impeach Donald Trump, the state party censured her, underscoring the extent to which her stance had fractured the once-unified front of Wyoming Republicans.

The censure motion, passed in February 2021, condemned Cheney for her impeachment vote, accusing her of disregarding the will of the Wyoming Republican Party and its voters. The repercussions were immediate, as Cheney faced not only a formal rebuke from the party but also a symbolic indication of the challenges she would encounter within her own political backyard.

Primary Challenges and the Wyoming Electorate:

The Wyoming Dilemma deepened as primary challenges emerged, fueled by the currents of Trumpism that had gained traction within the state. Political opponents, emboldened by the censure and seeking to capitalize on the divisions within the party, emerged as contenders for Cheney's congressional seat.

In the lead-up to the 2022 mid-term elections, Cheney found herself in a precarious position. Her principled stand, while earning accolades from a segment of the national conservative intelligentsia, collided head-on with the expectations and sentiments of a Wyoming electorate deeply connected to Trump's populist movement. The Wyoming Dilemma became a test not only of Cheney's political acumen but also of her ability to navigate the complex dynamics of Wyoming's political landscape.

Town Halls and Community Backlash:

As Cheney crisscrossed the state, engaging in town halls and community events, the Wyoming Dilemma unfolded in real-time. Town hall meetings, once forums for constituent engagement, became arenas where the complexities of her dissent played out. Wyomingites, known for their directness and forthrightness, voiced a spectrum of opinions that ranged from fervent support to vehement opposition.

The Wyoming Dilemma extended beyond policy disagreements to questions about loyalty, representation, and the expectations constituents had of their elected officials. The confrontations at town halls mirrored the broader fissures within the GOP, with Wyomingites grappling with the identity of their party and the role they envisioned for Wyoming within the national conservative movement.

The Echoes of the Past:

The Wyoming Dilemma was not merely a contemporary political struggle but also an echo of the Cheney family's past within the state. Wyomingites, who had witnessed the rise of Dick Cheney from their own ranks to the pinnacle of political power, now confronted the complexities of a new era. The legacy of the Cheney name, while a source of pride for many, became a double-edged sword as Liz Cheney navigated the expectations and comparisons that accompanied her family's storied history.

The echoes of the past extended to questions of political allegiance, as Wyomingites pondered whether Liz Cheney's allegiance lay with the traditional conservatism they embraced or with a broader vision that transcended the boundaries of the state. The interplay between familial legacy and individual conviction added layers of complexity to the Wyoming Dilemma, shaping the perceptions and judgments of constituents.

Navigating the Wyoming Dilemma:

As Liz Cheney grappled with the Wyoming Dilemma, her political navigation took on a character defined by resilience and an unwavering commitment to her principles. The challenge was not merely one of political survival but of finding a pathway that honored both her convictions and the expectations of her Wyoming constituents.

Town halls and community events, once emblematic of Wyoming's rugged democratic traditions, became arenas where the Wyoming Dilemma played out in nuanced and sometimes contentious ways. Cheney, with an iron will forged in the Wyoming wilderness, engaged directly with constituents, articulating her perspectives, and fielding questions that ran the gamut of political discourse.

The Wyoming Dilemma, while emblematic of broader trends within the GOP, became a microcosm of the challenges facing principled dissent within the party. Cheney's ability to navigate this dilemma would not only shape her political future but would also contribute to the evolving narrative of the Republican Party's identity in the post-Trump era.

As this chapter unfolds, the Wyoming Dilemma becomes a central theme in Liz Cheney's political journey. The challenges, complexities, and expectations that characterized her standing within the state showcase not only the dynamics of Wyoming politics but also the resilience of a leader determined to navigate the intricate terrain of dissent, loyalty, and the enduring quest for political integrity.

Chapter 13:

Legacy of Courage

Cheney Beyond Controversy: Reflecting on Liz Cheney's broader legacy and her influence on a new generation of conservative leaders.

As we navigate the turbulent waters of Liz Cheney's political journey, the Legacy of Courage emerges as a powerful undercurrent, shaping not only her personal narrative but also leaving an indelible mark on the broader landscape of American politics. Beyond the controversies that defined her recent years, this chapter serves as a reflection on Cheney's enduring legacy and her influence on a new generation of conservative leaders.

A Principled Voice in a Turbulent Era:

The Legacy of Courage finds its roots in Cheney's unyielding commitment to principles, even in the face of political storms. From her early years in Wyoming politics to the tumultuous events surrounding her stance against Trumpism, Cheney consistently demonstrated a rare form of political courage—an ability to navigate the complexities of a shifting political landscape while staying true to her convictions.

This legacy is deeply embedded in the very fabric of Cheney's political identity. It is evident in the moments when she stood alone, defying party norms for the sake of constitutional principles. The legacy is not merely one of dissent but of an unwavering belief that the foundations of democracy are worth defending, even when such a defense comes at a personal and political cost.

Navigating the Wyoming Dilemma:

The Legacy of Courage is perhaps most vividly illustrated in Cheney's response to the Wyoming Dilemma. As the political winds in her home state shifted, Cheney faced challenges that tested the mettle of her resolve. The Legacy of Courage, in this context, is not about avoiding controversy but about confronting it with an iron will and a commitment to enduring principles.

Cheney's navigation of the Wyoming Dilemma showcased a leader unafraid to engage directly with constituents, to face the complexities of dissent within her party, and to grapple with the expectations tied to her family's political legacy. The legacy being forged was one of resilience—a testament to the idea that courage extends beyond the halls of power and into the heart of communities.

Championing Constitutional Fidelity:

At the heart of the Legacy of Courage is Cheney's championing of constitutional fidelity in an era marked by political expediency. Her vocal condemnation of Donald Trump's actions, particularly in the aftermath of the Capitol riot, resonated as a call to preserve democratic norms and uphold the rule of law. The legacy is one of a leader who refused to be swayed by the prevailing winds of populism, choosing instead to anchor herself in the principles that have defined the American experiment.

This aspect of the legacy extends beyond partisan divides. Cheney's insistence on the importance of constitutional norms garnered respect from individuals across the political spectrum, from conservative intellectuals who saw in her a defender of conservative values to liberals who found common ground in the defense of democratic institutions.

Influence on a New Generation:

The Legacy of Courage is not confined to the individual journey of Liz Cheney; it extends to the broader impact she has had on a new generation of conservative leaders. Emerging from the crucible of internal party conflicts and ideological struggles, Cheney's influence reaches beyond the controversies that defined her tenure in the national spotlight.

Young conservatives, witnessing Cheney's principled stand, find in her a role model—a figure who stood against the currents of populism and prioritized principles over political expediency. The Legacy of Courage becomes a beacon for those navigating the complexities of a political landscape often defined by loyalty tests and ideological litmus tests.

Shaping the Narrative of Republican Dissent:

As we reflect on the Legacy of Courage, it becomes apparent that Cheney has played a pivotal role in shaping the narrative of dissent within the Republican Party. Her journey, marked by clashes with Trumpism and the fractures within the GOP, becomes a reference point for future leaders grappling with questions of loyalty, principles, and the enduring quest for political integrity.

The legacy extends to the broader conversation about the future of the Republican Party. Cheney, with her iron will and political brilliance, becomes a symbol of resistance against the tide of Trumpism, challenging the party to reckon with its identity and guiding it towards a path that transcends the personality cults that have defined recent political discourse.

A Woman Who Carved Her Own Path:

In the Legacy of Courage, Liz Cheney emerges not only as a defender of principles but as a woman who carved her own path in the halls of power. The legacy is about more than just political ideology; it is about breaking barriers and challenging the expectations placed on women in politics. Cheney's journey becomes a source of inspiration for women aspiring to leadership roles, illustrating that courage knows no gender and that resilience is a universal quality.

As we conclude this chapter, the Legacy of Courage stands as a testament to the enduring power of principles in the world of politics. Cheney's journey, marked by controversy, dissent, and an unwavering commitment to constitutional fidelity, becomes a chapter in the broader narrative of American political history. The legacy extends beyond the individual and becomes a touchstone for a new generation of leaders who, inspired by Cheney's courage, navigate the intricate terrain of contemporary politics with an iron will and an unwavering commitment to enduring principles.

Chapter 14:

The Future of the GOP

Post-Trump Landscape: Analyzing the evolving role of Liz Cheney in shaping the future trajectory of the Republican Party.

As we delve into the post-Trump landscape of American politics, the spotlight turns to one of its most consequential figures: Liz Cheney. Beyond the controversies and political battles that defined her recent years, Cheney emerges as a pivotal player in the intricate dance of reshaping the Republican Party. This chapter analyzes the evolving role of Liz Cheney and her impact on the future trajectory of the GOP.

The Shifting Sands of Republican Identity:

The post-Trump landscape presents the Republican Party with a complex set of challenges and opportunities. The era of Trumpism, marked by populist currents and a departure from traditional conservative norms, has left the GOP at a crossroads. As the party grapples with questions of identity, loyalty, and ideological coherence, Liz Cheney's role becomes increasingly central in navigating the shifting sands of Republican politics.

Cheney's dissent against Trump's influence within the party has positioned her as a symbol of resistance against the populist tide. Her commitment to constitutional principles and her refusal to be swayed by the prevailing winds of political expediency distinguish her as a unique voice within the GOP. The question that looms large is whether Cheney's influence will help guide the party back to its conservative roots or if the populist forces that gained prominence during the Trump era will continue to define its path.

The Guardian of Conservative Principles:

Cheney's role as the guardian of conservative principles comes to the forefront as the GOP navigates its post-Trump future. Traditional conservatives, who have long been the bedrock of the party, find in Cheney a champion for the enduring values that have defined conservatism for decades. Her unwavering commitment to constitutional fidelity and the rule of law resonates with those who believe that the party should be rooted in principles rather than personality.

In the evolving landscape, Cheney's influence becomes a counterweight to the populist currents that have reshaped the GOP. The tension between these two ideological currents becomes a defining feature of the party's future, with Cheney emerging as a symbol of a conservatism that transcends the cult of personality.

Cheney's Leadership in the House:

As the GOP looks to the future, Cheney's leadership role in the House of Representatives takes on heightened significance. Despite facing challenges within her own party, including the removal from her leadership position, Cheney's continued presence in the House provides a platform to shape the narrative and direction of the GOP.

Her strategic positioning within the House Republican Conference allows her to influence the legislative agenda, rally support for conservative principles, and challenge narratives that veer away from constitutional norms. Cheney's role in the House becomes a focal point for those within the party seeking a return to a conservatism anchored in principles rather than a blind allegiance to a single leader.

Navigating Primary Challenges:

The post-Trump landscape is characterized by primary challenges that reflect the ongoing struggle for the soul of the GOP. Cheney, facing primary opponents endorsed by Trump and his allies, becomes a barometer for the battle between traditional conservatism and Trumpism at the grassroots level.

The outcomes of these primary contests will have far-reaching implications for the future trajectory of the GOP. Cheney's ability to navigate and potentially overcome these challenges will signal whether the party is willing to embrace a diversity of voices or if it will continue down a path defined by loyalty tests and ideological conformity.

The Role of Cheney's Allies:

As Cheney charts the future of the GOP, her alliances with fellow Republicans who share her commitment to conservative principles become crucial. Senators like Mitt Romney and Ben Sasse, along with other House Republicans who have stood by her side, amplify the influence of a conservative bloc within the party.

The collaboration between Cheney and like-minded allies shapes the narrative of dissent within the GOP. Their collective influence extends beyond individual disagreements with Trump and becomes emblematic of a broader movement seeking to reassert traditional conservative values within the party.

The Specter of Trump's Influence:

The future of the GOP is inexorably linked to the specter of Trump's influence. The question of whether the party will continue to be defined by the former president's populist brand or if it will undergo a recalibration towards principled conservatism remains unanswered.

Cheney's role in shaping the future trajectory of the GOP hinges on her ability to navigate the delicate dance between acknowledging the impact of Trumpism and advocating for a return to core conservative values. Her willingness to confront the challenges posed by Trump's influence while maintaining her commitment to principles becomes a defining feature of her role in the post-Trump landscape.

Public Perception and the Media Landscape:

The evolving narrative around Liz Cheney is intricately woven into the broader media landscape and public perception of the GOP. Cheney's public statements, media appearances, and engagement with the press contribute to shaping the narrative of dissent and the future of the party.

As a prominent voice in the post-Trump GOP, Cheney's interactions with the media become a lens through which the public gauges the direction of the Republican Party. Her ability to articulate a vision for the GOP that goes beyond personality cults and prioritizes enduring principles will be crucial in shaping public perception.

Conclusion: Forging a Path Forward:

As we conclude our analysis of Liz Cheney's role in shaping the future of the GOP, the trajectory of the party remains uncertain. The post-Trump landscape is a terrain fraught with ideological tensions, power struggles, and questions about the soul of the Republican Party.

Cheney's legacy, rooted in a commitment to constitutional principles and an unwavering defiance against Trumpism, becomes a guidepost for those within the GOP seeking to forge a path forward. The future of the GOP is entwined with the choices the party makes in navigating the delicate balance between loyalty to a charismatic leader and a return to principled conservatism.

As Cheney continues to play a central role in the House and the broader political discourse, her influence on the trajectory of the GOP will be a story told not just in the halls of power but also in the hearts and minds of Republicans grappling with the choices that will define the party's future. The chapter concludes, leaving the reader on the precipice of a political landscape where the future of the GOP hangs in the balance, with Liz Cheney at the center of a complex and evolving narrative.

Chapter 15:

The Unfinished Story

Continuing the Journey: Speculating on Liz Cheney's future in American politics and the enduring impact of her defiant stand against Trumpism.

As we stand at the threshold of the concluding chapter of Liz Cheney's biographical journey, the narrative is far from complete. The Unfinished Story unfolds, inviting readers into the realm of speculation, foresight, and the tantalizing question of what lies ahead for a woman who has defied convention, challenged power, and carved her own path in the halls of political power.

A Defiant Legacy:

The Unfinished Story of Liz Cheney is, in many ways, a testament to her defiant legacy. As we look back at the turbulent years that defined her public persona, it becomes evident that Cheney's story is one of resilience, courage, and an unyielding commitment to principles. The defiance against the currents of Trumpism, the willingness to stand alone in the face of party censure, and the relentless pursuit of constitutional fidelity have etched Cheney's name into the annals of American political history.

The Unfinished Story examines how this legacy of defiance will continue to reverberate through the corridors of power, shaping the conversations around conservatism, loyalty, and the very soul of the Republican Party. The question that lingers is whether Cheney's defiance will be a standalone chapter or a prelude to a broader movement within the GOP.

The Trajectory of Leadership:

Speculating on Liz Cheney's future in American politics invites us to consider the trajectory of her leadership. The Unfinished Story is a canvas upon which the potential roles and responsibilities that Cheney may assume unfold. Will she continue to be a guiding voice within the House, rallying a conservative bloc around enduring principles? Or does the future hold a different path, one that takes her beyond the legislative chambers and into the realm of broader political influence?

Cheney's leadership style, characterized by an iron will and a commitment to principled conservatism, positions her as a figure capable of shaping the narrative of dissent within the GOP. The Unfinished Story raises the possibility that Cheney's leadership may extend beyond the confines of the House of Representatives, influencing the broader trajectory of the Republican Party in ways yet to be fully realized.

Challenges and Opportunities:

The Unfinished Story acknowledges that Liz Cheney's journey is marked by both challenges and opportunities. The challenges, epitomized by primary contests and party censure, speak to the tensions within the GOP. The Unfinished Story poses the question of whether Cheney's principled stand will be a rallying point for those seeking a return to conservative roots or if the populist forces that have defined recent years will continue to hold sway.

Opportunities, on the other hand, present themselves in the form of alliances with like-minded conservatives, strategic positioning within the party, and the ongoing battle for the narrative of Republican identity. The Unfinished Story explores how Cheney's ability to navigate these challenges and seize opportunities will play a pivotal role in determining her impact on the future landscape of American politics.

A Symbol of Resistance:

Liz Cheney's defiant stand against Trumpism positions her as a symbol of resistance within the GOP. The Unfinished Story considers the enduring impact of this symbolism. Will Cheney's legacy become emblematic of a broader movement within the party, challenging the prevailing winds of populism and advocating for a conservatism anchored in enduring principles?

The symbolism of resistance is not merely a footnote in Cheney's story but a central theme that resonates with conservatives seeking to reclaim the soul of the Republican Party. The Unfinished Story speculates on whether Cheney's influence will transcend individual political battles and become a touchstone for those within the GOP navigating the complexities of loyalty, dissent, and the enduring quest for political integrity.

Legacy Beyond Politics:

As we peer into the future outlined in The Unfinished Story, it becomes evident that Liz Cheney's impact extends beyond the realm of politics. The Unfinished Story speculates on whether her legacy will transcend the partisan divides and resonate with a broader audience—those who value courage, resilience, and an unwavering commitment to constitutional principles.

Cheney's story, as The Unfinished Story suggests, may inspire future leaders, especially women, to carve their own paths in the often challenging landscape of American politics. The legacy beyond politics is one that reflects the indomitable spirit of a woman who, against formidable odds, stood firm in her convictions and defied the prevailing winds of political expediency.

A Narrative Yet to Unfold:

As we draw the curtain on The Unfinished Story, it becomes clear that Liz Cheney's journey is a narrative yet to unfold fully. The speculations, anticipations, and questions raised within this chapter are signposts on a road that leads into the uncharted territories of American politics. The Unfinished Story leaves readers in suspense, contemplating the possibilities and potentialities that lie ahead for a woman who has become a singular figure in the contemporary political landscape.

The future of Liz Cheney is an open book, waiting to be written with each passing day, each political maneuver, and each principled stand. The Unfinished Story is a reminder that the journey of a political figure extends beyond the confines of a single biography—it is a story that continues to evolve, leaving an indelible mark on the pages of history. The concluding chapter, like the chapters that preceded it, serves as a testament to the enduring nature of Liz Cheney's impact and the narrative that is yet to reach its final resolution.

Conclusion: Defiance, Legacy, and the Power of Conviction

As we draw the curtain on the pages of "Liz Cheney: The Woman Who Took on Trump," the narrative echoes with the resonance of defiance, resilience, and the indomitable spirit of a woman who carved her own path in the tumultuous halls of power. Liz Cheney's journey, illuminated in the preceding chapters, transcends the boundaries of political biography—it becomes a beacon of inspiration for all who dare to challenge the status quo and stand firm in their convictions.

In the crucible of political battles, Cheney emerged as a symbol of resistance against the prevailing winds of Trumpism. Her story is not just a chronicle of clashes with a former president; it is a testament to the enduring power of individual conviction. As we navigate the complex terrain of contemporary politics, Cheney's legacy serves as a reminder that principles, anchored in the bedrock of constitutional fidelity, can withstand the storms of ideological tumult.

The iron will and political brilliance that define Cheney's narrative are not merely attributes of a singular figure; they are a call to action for every reader. In her journey, we find the courage to defy the expectations, to challenge the norms, and to forge our own paths. Cheney's story becomes a catalyst for embracing the discomfort of dissent, acknowledging the power of an individual's voice in the broader tapestry of democracy.

Beyond the clashes with Trump, beyond the fractures within the GOP, lies the enduring legacy of a woman who refused to compromise on her principles. The reader is invited to reflect on their own convictions, to find the courage to speak truth to power, and to navigate the complexities of contemporary politics with an unwavering commitment to enduring values.

As we close this biographical chapter on Liz Cheney, let it serve as a motivational parable for those who aspire to make a difference. Whether in the political arena or the broader landscape of life, Cheney's story teaches us that the pursuit of integrity, the adherence to principles, and the willingness to face the uncomfortable truths are the hallmarks of transformative leadership.

In every moment of challenge, in every clash with adversity, remember the woman who took on Trump. Remember the iron will that withstood the storms, the political brilliance that illuminated the darkest corners, and the unyielding commitment to oath and honor that became a guiding light. Let Liz Cheney's story inspire a new generation of leaders, activists, and citizens who dare to imagine a future shaped by the power of conviction.

As you close this book, carry with you the lessons of defiance, the echoes of an extraordinary journey, and the motivation to forge your own path. Let Liz Cheney's legacy not be confined to the pages of this biography but become a living testament to the enduring impact of courage, resilience, and the unwavering pursuit of truth.

Now, dear reader, go forth with the spirit of Liz Cheney as your companion. Embrace the challenges, question the norms, and let your convictions be the guiding stars in the vast expanse of your journey. The halls of power may be tumultuous, but within you lies the power to shape the narrative, to challenge the status quo, and to leave an indelible mark on the pages of history. The woman who took on Trump beckons you to write your own story of defiance, brilliance, and a legacy that transcends the ordinary.

Made in the USA
Middletown, DE
21 October 2024